THE CANTERVILLE GHOST

OSCAR WILDE

THE CANTERVILLE GHOST

The vocabulary is based on
Michael West: A General Service List of
English Words, revised & enlarged edition, 1953
Pacemaker Core Vocabulary, 1975
Salling/Hvid: English-Danish Basic Dictionary, 1970
J. A. van Ek: The Threshold Level for Modern Language
Learning in Schools, 1976

EDITORS:
Aage Salling, *Denmark*
Erik Hvid, *Denmark*
Revised edition by Robert Dewsnap, 1980

Series editors: Ulla Malmmose
and Charlotte Bistrup

Cover layout: Mette Plesner
Cover photo: Jess Vallarino

Illustrations: Oskar Jørgensen

Easy Readers

EGMONT

Printed in Denmark

1

Canterville Chase

Mr Hiram B. Otis, the important American, came to buy *Canterville Chase*. Everyone told him that it was not a very good idea. Everyone knew that there was a *ghost* in the place. Lord Canterville said he must tell Mr Otis about it; this was when he came to talk about the money.

"I must tell you, Mr Otis," he said. "Many living people have seen the ghost. And we do not want to live at Canterville Chase any longer. He *scared* my *sister* very badly. He put his hands on her arms while she was dressing. After

---

ghost: see picture, page 12
scare, make afraid
my *sister,* woman (or girl) with the same father and mother as I

that, none of our younger *servants* wanted to stay with us in the *castle*. There were sounds from the *corridor* and from some of the rooms at night. Often Lady Canterville could not sleep."

"My Lord," answered Mr Otis, "I come not from an old country but from America. We don't believe in ghosts. I'll take the castle and I'll pay what you want for it."

"I am almost sure that the ghost is there," said Lord Canterville. "People have known it for three hundred years. It always comes before someone in the castle dies."

"So does the family doctor, Lord Canterville; but there is no such thing as a ghost."

"If you don't mind a ghost in the house, all right. But now I have told you about it."

A few weeks after this, Mr Otis and his family went down to Canterville Chase. There were Mr Otis himself; his wife, a beautiful New York lady; Washington, their eldest son; Virginia, a little girl of fifteen; and two *twin* boys.

servant

---

castle, very large old house
corridor, long room between other rooms
twin, of the same age and with the same mother

Canterville Chase is seven miles from the nearest *railway station*. Mr Otis had asked for a *carriage* to meet them. It was a fine July evening, and the sky was blue. But as they drove up to the castle, a number of big black birds flew over their heads. The sky grew dark, and some big drops of rain began to fall.

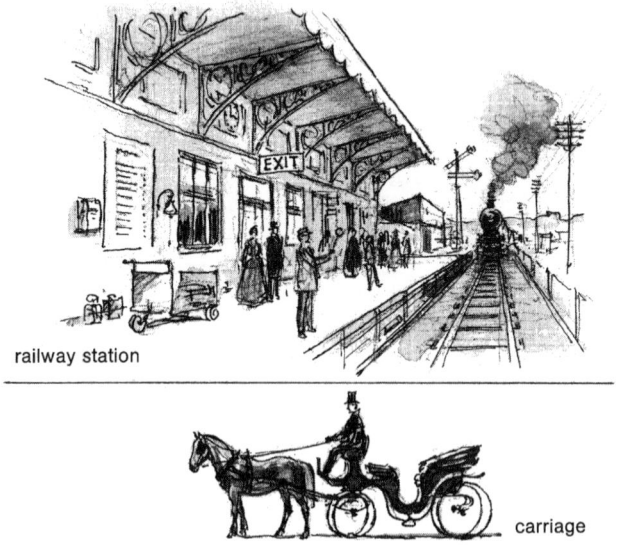

railway station

carriage

An old woman was standing on the steps to receive them. This was Mrs Umney, who kept the house in order. "I hope you will like it at Canterville Chase," she said. They followed her into the house, and came into a long, low room with a large window. Here they sat down and looked around, while *Mrs Umney served them tea.*

"Look at the floor there," said Mrs Otis. She pointed to a large red *stain.*

"Yes," said Mrs Umney, "that is blood."

"I don't like that," Mrs Otis went on. "Someone must take it away at once."

"It is the blood of Lady Eleanore Canterville.

Mrs Umney served them tea   stain

She was the wife of Sir Simon Canterville. She was his wife, but he killed her – right here – in 1575. He lived here for nine years after she died; and then no-one ever saw him again. At least, not living. But his ghost still walks about the castle. No-one can take the blood-stain away."

"Yes, they can," said Mr Otis. "I have something here that will take it away." Before the old woman could stop him, he took out a small black stick and put it to the stain. "Now it is gone," he said. "I knew I could do it."

flash of
lightning

stick

But as he said these words a *flash of lightning* filled the room with a strong light. Then, a *peal of thunder* travelled through the house. They all jumped to their feet. "I have seen many things here with my own eyes," said Mrs Umney. "Some of them would make your hair stand on end. Many nights I have not closed an eye, such *awful things* happen here."

Mr and Mrs Otis just told her that they were not afraid of ghosts. Then Mrs Umney left the family to go to her own room.

---

peal of thunder, deep sound after a flash of lightning
awful things, things that made her afraid

Questions

1. Where is Canterville Chase?
2. Why is Mr Otis not afraid of ghosts?
3. What is the weather like when they arrive?
4. Why is the blood-stain there?
5. What happens when Mr Otis has taken away the blood-stain?

2

There was thunder and lightning all that night. The next morning, when they came down to breakfast, they found the *terrible* blood-stain on the floor again. "I have tried to take it away," said Washington. "It must be the ghost." He took away the stain again, but the second morning it was there again. That evening, *Mr Otis locked the door* and took the key away with him. But the third morning, too, the stain was there again. The whole family were interested now.

Mr Otis locked the door

terrible, awful

The day was nice and warm. In the evening the family went out for a drive in the carriage. They did not come home till nine o'clock. Then they ate. At eleven o'clock they went to bed, and by half past eleven all the lights were out. Some time later, Mr Otis heard a strange sound in the corridor outside his room. He got up to see what time it was. It was one o'clock. The *noise* did not stop, and now he heard footsteps. He opened the door, and there he saw a terrible old man. Long white hair fell down from his head, his eyes were like fire, and heavy chains were on his hands and feet.

the Canterville Ghost

chains

"My dear sir," said Mr Otis, "you must not make such a noise. Here is some *oil* for your chains. I shall leave it here in the corridor and I shall give you more later." And with these

noise, sound
oil, something in a bottle to make chains quiet

words Mr Otis closed his door and went back to bed.

For a short time the Canterville ghost stood quite still. Then he threw the bottle on the floor and ran down the corridor. An awful green light came from him. He came to the end of the corridor; and then – a door *quietly* opened and someone threw a large *pillow* at his head. He had to get away – so he went through the wall. And the house became *quiet* again.

When he came to his small room in the left *wing* of the castle, he sat down to think. Never before had anybody done such things to him.

He thought of all the great things he had done. Once, he scared Lord Canterville's sister very badly. Another time, he *grinned* at four

pillow

---

quiet, quietly, without noise
wing: see picture, page 14
grin, smile with open mouth

wing

girls through a window; they ran away and never came back. One morning, he sat in an old woman's chair; she saw him and was *ill* in bed for a long time. Later, a servant killed himself with a *revolver*; this was because he saw a green hand on the window. All these great things came back to him, and now these Americans gave him oil for his chains and threw pillows at his head. He certainly had to do something. All night long, he thought about what to do.

revolver

---

ill, not well

Questions

1. Who tries to take away the blood-stain?
2. What does Mr Otis hear in the corridor?
3. What does the ghost look like?
4. What does the ghost think of the Americans?

3

The next morning at breakfast, the Otis family talked about the ghost. "I am very sorry he did not want the oil for his chains," said Mr Otis. "If he does not use it, we must take his chains from him. And it is not at all nice of you to throw pillows at his head," Mr Otis went on. He was speaking to the twins, who began to laugh.

For the rest of the week they saw nothing of the ghost. They only saw the blood-stain. This came out again every morning, but never in the same colour. There was only one person who did not laugh when they talked about the ghost. This was little Virginia. She was very *sad* when she saw the blood-stain. *Tears* came to her eyes one morning when it was quite green.

One Sunday night, just after they had gone to bed, they heard a *frightful* noise in the hall. They ran down to look. A large *suit of armour* had fallen on the *stone floor*. Sitting in a high chair was the Canterville ghost. Mr Otis took out his revolver and told the ghost to hold up his hands. The ghost jumped up with a cry and ran past them. He put out the light and left

---

sad, sorry
tears, water (in the eyes of a sad person)
frightful, terrible, awful

suit of armour.

stone

stone floor

them in the dark. At the top of the steps he stopped and gave a terrible laugh. It sounded through the large, high room for several long moments. A door opened, and Mrs Otis came out. "I am afraid you are not well," she said. "Here is a bottle. Drink this and you will feel better."

The ghost looked at her, very angry now; and he began to turn himself into a big black dog. But he stopped this when he heard the sound of footsteps. The twins came up to him, but they found only a spot of green light moving out through the wall.

In his room he sat down, very sad. A ghost in armour! What a good idea to scare the family! It was his own suit of armour, too. *Queen Elizabeth* herself had said that she liked it very much. But when he had put it on, it was too heavy for

---

Queen Elizabeth, Elizabeth I, Queen of England and Ireland 1558-1603

him. So he had fallen on the floor and hit his leg.

For some days he was very ill, and only left his room to keep the blood-stain in order. Then, he decided to try once more to scare the family. How about Friday the 13th of August? In the evening it began to rain, and the wind was so strong that all the doors and windows made a noise. He liked that.

His plan was this: first, to go to Washington's room and make awful noises from the foot of the boy's bed; and then *to put a knife* three times slowly *through his own head* to the sound of music. Next, to go into the room of the American and his wife, and put a cold hand on Mrs Otis's head; and to say terrible things into Mr Otis's ear. He did not know what to do to little Virginia; she was a nice girl, and had never done anything to him. But then there were the

to put a knife through his own head

twins. The first thing, of course, was to sit on them; this would give them bad *dreams*. Then he would go down on the floor and go once round their bed. He would look at them with one big, green eye; and laugh until they were quite badly scared.

---

dreams, pictures as they sleep

At half past ten he listened: the family were going to bed. He could hear the twins laughing and making a noise; but at a quarter past eleven all was still. He stepped out of the wall with a grin on his face; then he walked down the corridor towards Washington's door. He laughed to himself and turned the corner. And there he fell back against the wall. He put his long hands to his white face: there in front of him was a frightful ghost. It had no hair; its face was round and white. There was an awful grin on its face, and fire came out of its mouth. From the eyes came a strong red light, and in its right hand was a heavy *sword*. The Canterville ghost was very much afraid. He had never seen a ghost before. So he turned round and ran back to his room as fast as he could.

sword

All night he lay on his bed, white and scared. Just before morning, he went back to the same place again. After all, two ghosts were better than one. Perhaps it was a friend, to help him against the twins.

But what he saw was terrible. The other ghost was standing against the wall. The light had gone out of its eyes and the sword had fallen from its hand. When the Canterville ghost took it by the arm, it fell to the floor. And there was the Canterville ghost holding in his

turnip

broom

arms a pillow, a *broom,* a *turnip* and a paper with some words written on it.

The twins were playing a game with him. The old Canterville look came into his eyes; he lifted his hand towards their door. It meant "I shall come back." Then he moved away to his room.

Questions

1. How does Virginia feel about the ghost?

2. What do they find when they go down at one o'clock?

3. What does Mrs Otis say to the ghost?

4. Why does the Canterville ghost run away from the other ghost?

5. What is the other ghost?

4

For five whole days he did not leave his room. He did not even keep the blood-stain in order. The Otis family did not want it; so he was not going to look after it any more. But he had to walk in the corridor one night every week. And he had to make his frightful noises from the large window in the east; this was on the first and third Wednesday in every month. True, his life had not been good at all; but as a ghost he did do his job well.

For the next three Saturdays he walked down the corridor, between 12 o'clock and 3 o'clock at night. But he did his best not to make any noise. He took off his *boots* and oiled his

boot

chains – he had taken the bottle of oil from Mr Otis's bedroom while the family were at table.

Still the twins did not leave him alone. They put up *strings* across the corridor. They put out oil on the floor. And one night he fell on his right arm. This made him very angry. So he decided to go to the boys' room the next night as The Man Without A Head.

string

At eleven o'clock he began to get ready. He dressed and put on his big boots. Then he found his *pistols*. At a quarter past one he came out of the wall and walked down the corridor. When he came to the twins' room, he found the door half open. He stopped – then he opened it and went in. There was a noise, and a heavy *bucket* of water fell down on top of him. It made him wet to the skin, and it nearly fell on his right arm. At

---

pistol, bucket: see picture, page 26

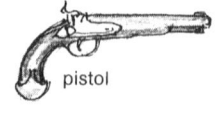
pistol

bucket

the same time he heard a laugh from the big bed. He ran back to his room as fast as he could. The next day he did not feel at all well and had to stay in bed. It was a good thing he had not taken his head with him to the twins' room!

He now no longer even hoped to scare the family. He was always very quiet when he walked up and down in the house. But the twins did not leave him alone. One night he went down to look at the blood-stain. After that, he stood and looked at the family pictures on the wall. Suddenly, the two boys jumped out at him and cried "BOO!" in his ear. He ran up to the corridor. And there he met Washington,

who was waiting for him with a big garden-*syringe*. The only way for him to run away was through the wall.

After this, the family did not see him again. Everybody thought that he had gone away. Mrs Otis gave a big party; Mr Otis began to write a book; the twins played in the garden. And Virginia rode about the fields on her little horse with a friend of hers, a young man. He was at Canterville for the last week of his holidays.

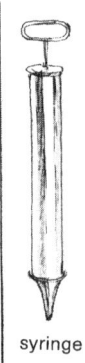

syringe

Questions

1. What is the ghost's job?
2. Why does he fall in the corridor?
3. What happens when he goes into the twins' room?
4. How does he run away from Washington?

5

One day when Virginia and her friend came back from a ride on their horses, she went up by a back door. She did not want anybody to see her. As she was running down the corridor, she saw someone in a bedroom. The door was open, and she looked in to see who it was. And there was the Canterville ghost himself! He was sitting by the window, looking at the trees in

the garden outside. Virginia's first idea was to run away. But he looked so sad that she felt sorry for him. So she went in to speak to him. She was very quiet, and he only heard her when she spoke to him.

"I'm sorry for you," she said. "But tomorrow my brothers are going away. And then, if you are a good ghost, we shall all leave you alone."

"Don't ask me to be good. I must walk about at night, if that is what you mean," answered the ghost. "That is why I am here."

"Perhaps," she said, "but you have been very bad. Mrs Umney told us on our first day that you killed your wife."

"Well, that is true," said the ghost. "But it was a family matter, and only the family should talk about it. No other persons had anything to do with it."

"It is very wrong to kill anyone," said Virginia.

"My wife was not beautiful, she did not look after my clothes, and she was no good in the kitchen. But it is all past now. Her brothers let me *starve to death*. That was not very nice of them, even if I did kill her."

"Oh, Mr Ghost – I mean Sir Simon! Do you want something to eat?"

---

starve to death, die because there was no food

"No thank you, I never eat anything now. But it is very good of you; you are much nicer than the rest of your terrible family."

"Stop!" cried Virginia, and *stamped her foot*. "It is you who are terrible. You took the colours out of my box to keep that blood-stain in order. And you know it! You took all my reds and yellows and greens – yes, all my colours. I shall go to my father and ask him to keep the twins at home for another week!"

"Please don't go, Miss Virginia," he cried. "I

Virginia stamped her foot

am so sad; I don't know what to do. I want to go to sleep and I cannot."

"Of course you can. You just go to bed and put out the light," said Virginia.

"I have not slept for three hundred years," he said sadly. "For three hundred years I have not slept, and I am tired."

Virginia came up to him and looked into his old face. "Poor, poor ghost," she said. "Have you no place where you can sleep?"

"There is a garden behind the woods. There the *grass* grows long and the *birds* sing all night; all night they sing; it would be good to sleep there."

"You mean the Garden of Death?" she asked.

grass
bird

"Yes, *Death*. Death must be beautiful. To lie in the kind, brown earth with the grass growing

---

Death: Death comes when a person dies

over one's head – and peace and quiet! To have no yesterday and no tomorrow, to forget time, to forget life. You can help me. You can open Death's door to me, for Love is always with you; and love is stronger than Death."

Virginia turned white in the face, and she shook all over. She felt she was in a terrible dream.

The ghost spoke again: "Have you ever read the *verse* on the window? In the room where the blood-stain is?"

"Oh, often!" cried the little girl, looking up. "I know it quite well. There are only six lines:

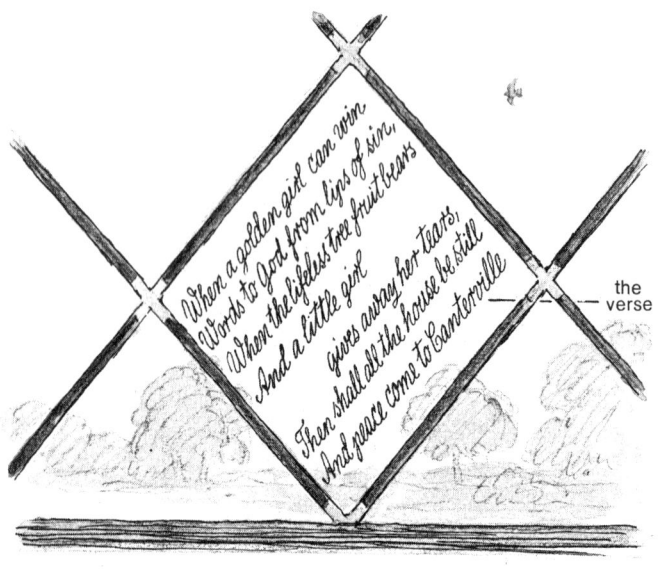

When a golden girl can win,
Words to God from lips of sin,
When the lifeless tree fruit bears,
And a little girl
gives away her tears,
Then shall all the house be still
And peace come to Canterville

the verse

"But I don't know what they mean," Virginia said.

"They mean," said the ghost, "that you must give tears for me, because I have no tears. And help me to *pray* to *God,* because I don't believe in God. And then, if you have been good, Death will be good to me. You will see terrible things, but it will not matter to you. Your love is too great for them."

The ghost looked down at Virginia's golden head. After some time she stood up. "I will come," she said. "I am not afraid."

He kissed her hand

He got up and took her hand and kissed it. His fingers were as cold as ice, and the kiss burned like fire. But Virginia was not afraid as he walked with her through the dark room. She felt the pictures on the walls looking at her.

---

pray, talk to *God*
God, the father who made the world

35

They seemed to say, "Go back, little girl! Go back!" But Virginia did not go back. When they came to the other end of the room, the ghost stopped. He said some words she could not hear. Then she saw the wall open. A cold wind came out. "Quick, quick," cried the ghost, "or it will be too late." And then the wall closed behind them, and the room was empty.

Questions

1. Why does Virginia go in by the back door?

2. Where does she see the Canterville ghost?

3. Why did Sir Simon kill his wife?

4. Does the ghost want something to eat?

5. What does he want?

6. How will Virginia help him?

6

About ten minutes later the Otis family came down to have tea. As Virginia did not come down, Mrs Otis sent the twins up to find her. Virginia often went out to pick flowers for the table, so Mrs Otis was not troubled about her.

But at six o'clock she had still not come back. So Mrs Otis sent the boys out again to look for her. She herself and Mr Otis looked in every room in the house. They were all very much afraid now. Mr Otis asked the police to look out for little Virginia. Then he asked the family to sit down to eat. He told a servant to bring round his horse, and he rode down the Ascot Road. After a few minutes, he heard a horse behind him, and looked round. He saw Virginia's friend, Cecil, coming up very fast.

"I'm very sorry, Mr Otis," he said. "But I can't eat anything until Virginia is found. You won't send me back, will you? I can't go! I won't go!"

"Well, Cecil, if you won't go back then you must come along with me."

They rode on quickly to the railway station, but nobody there had seen Virginia. At eleven o'clock they came back, very tired and very sad. They found Washington and the twins waiting for them on the road. They, too, had been looking for Virginia, but they had not found her.

In the castle, Mr Otis told them all to go to bed. He said that they could do nothing more that night.

Just as they were coming out of the sitting-room they heard the clock strike twelve. A frightful peal of thunder shook the whole house. Part of the wall at the top of the steps opened with a loud noise; and Virginia came out, very white in the face, with a small box in her hand. They ran up to her, and Mrs Otis, with tears in her eyes, took her in her arms.

"Where have you been, child?" asked Mr Otis. "We have been looking for you everywhere."

"Thank God you are here," said Mrs Otis. "But you must never leave us like that again."

"Father, I have been with the ghost. He is dead, and you must come and see him. He had

been a very bad man. But he was sorry for all that he had done. And he gave me this beautiful box before he died."

The whole family just looked at her – they

could not say a word. After some time, Virginia turned round and walked through the opening in the wall. She then went down a corridor, and the rest of the family followed. At the end of the corridor there was a heavy door. Virginia put her hand on it. It opened, and they found themselves in a little room with one small window. In the wall there was a heavy ring with chains hanging down from it. And in the chains they saw a *skeleton*. Virginia put her little hands together and looked at it. And the others looked at it too, in great surprise.

skeleton

"Oh, look!" cried one of the twins, looking out of the window. "The old tree under the sitting-room window is green again. And I can see apples on it."

"God is not angry with him any more," said Virginia. As she spoke, the others looked at her. And it seemed to them that there was a beautiful light in her face.

Questions

1. Why is Mrs Otis not troubled about Virginia at first?

2. Where do Mr Otis and Cecil go to find Virginia?

3. What does Virginia look like when she comes?

4. What does Virginia show them?

Four days later they took Sir Simon to the Garden of Death. At eleven o'clock at night four carriages started from Canterville Chase. Lord Canterville was there, Mr and Mrs Otis, Washington and the twins, and Virginia. And in the last carriage was Mrs Umney.

They put him in a deep *grave*. It was in a corner of the Garden, under an old tree. Virginia

grave

flower

covered his grave with *flowers*. As she did so the moon came out, and the birds began to sing. She remembered what the ghost had said about the Garden of Death. Her eyes filled with tears. She could not say a word on the way back to the castle.

The next morning, before Lord Canterville went up to town, Mr Otis spoke with him.

"My Lord," he said, "here are some jewels. They were in the box that Sir Simon gave Virginia. It is quite clear to me that these jewels should be in your family. Virginia is too young

jewel box

jewels

for them. Perhaps you will let her have the box. It would make her very happy."

"My dear sir," answered Lord Canterville,

"your daughter was very kind to Sir Simon. My family is very thankful for what she did for him. The jewels are hers. If I take them away from her, the old man will be out of his grave again in two weeks. The castle is yours, and so is everything in it."

Mr Otis was sorry that Lord Canterville did not want to take the jewels. He asked him to think it over again. But the answer was no. And on the day when Virginia was married to young Cecil, she wore the jewels. Everybody thought how beautiful they were.

On the afternoon of that happy day, Virginia and Cecil walked down to the Garden of Death to look at Sir Simon's grave. "Virginia," said Cecil, "there is something you should tell me."

"What is that, Cecil dear?"

"You have never told me what happened that day. The day when you were in that room alone with the ghost."

"I have never told anyone," she said.

"I know, but perhaps you can tell me."

"Don't ask me, Cecil. I cannot tell you. Poor Sir Simon! He made me see what Life is, and what Death is; and why Love is stronger than both."

"You need not tell me as long as I have your heart."

"You have always had that, Cecil."

"And you will tell our children some day, won't you?"

Virginia turned red.

Questions

1. How many people go to the Garden of Death?

2. Why doesn't Lord Canterville take the jewels?

3. What has Virginia learnt from Sir Simon?

4. Why does Virginia turn red?

www.easyreaders.eu

IRREGULAR VERBS

be, was/ *pl* were, been
bear, bore, borne
become, became, become
begin, began, begun
blow, blew, blown
break, broke, broken
build, built, built
buy, bought, bought
can, could, (been able to)
catch, caught, caught
come, came, come
cost, cost, cost
cut, cut, cut
dig, dug, dug
do, did, done
draw, drew, drawn
drink, drank, drunk
drive, drove, driven
eat, ate, eaten
fall, fell, fallen
feel, felt, felt
fight, fought, fought
find, found, found
fly, flew, flown
forget, forgot, forgotten
get, got, got
give, gave, given
go, went, gone
grow, grew, grown
hang, hung, hung
have, had, had
hear, heard, heard
hit, hit, hit
hold, held, held
keep, kept, kept
lay, laid, laid
lead, led, led
learn, learnt/learned, learnt/learned
leave, left, left
let, let, let
lie, lay, lain

light, lit/lighted, lit/lighted
lose, lost, lost
make, made, made
may, might, (been allowed to)
mean, meant, meant
meet, met, met
must, must, (had to)
pay, paid, paid
put, put, put
read, read, read
ride, rode, ridden
ring, rang, rung
rise, rose, risen
run, ran, run
say, said, said
see, saw, seen
sell, sold, sold
send, sent, sent
set, set, set
shake, shook, shaken
shall, should, (been obliged to)
show, showed, shown
sing, sang, sung
sit, sat, sat
sleep, slept, slept
speak, spoke, spoken
spend, spent, spent
stand, stood, stood
strike, struck, struck
swim, swam, swum
take, took, taken
teach, taught, taught
tell, told, told
think, thought, thought
throw, threw, thrown
wear, wore, worn
will, would, (wanted to)
win, won, won
wind, wound, wound
write, wrote, written

EASY READERS *Denmark*
ERNST KLETT SPRACHEN *Germany*
ARCOBALENO *Spain*
LIBER *Sweden*
PRACTICUM EDUCATIEF BV. *Holland*
EUROPEAN SCHOOLBOOKS PUBLISHING LTD. *UK and Eire*
WYDAWNICTWO LEKTORKLETT *Poland*
KLETT KIADO KFT. *Hungary*
NÜANS PUBLISHING *Turkey*
ALLECTO LTD. *Estonia*
EMC CORP. *USA*

EASY READER TITLES NOW AVAILABLE:
Sir Arthur Conan Doyle: The Red Circle (A)
Sir Arthur Conan Doyle: The Speckled Band (A)
Lois Lowry: Number the Stars (A)
R. L. Stine: Stay Out of the Basement (A)
R. L. Stevenson: The Bottle Imp (A)
Oscar Wilde: The Canterville Ghost (A)
Oscar Wilde: The Canterville Ghost, dramatized version (A)
Enid Blyton: Five on a Treasure Island (B)
Roald Dahl: The Way up to Heaven and Other Stories (B)
Sir Arthur Conan Doyle: Black Peter - The Red-Headed League (B)
Lois Duncan: I know what you did last Summer (B)
Lois Duncan: Killing Mr. Griffin (B)
James Herriot: If Only They Could Talk (B)
Colin Higgins: Harold and Maude (B)
S.E. Hinton: The Outsiders (B)
Jerome K. Jerome: Three Men in a Boat (B)
Ira Levin: The Stepford Wives (B)
Pat Lowe: The Girl with No Name (B)
Brian Moore: Lies of Silence (B)
R. L. Stine: Fear Street: The Perfect Date (B)
Mark Twain: Tom Sawyer (B)
Oscar Wilde: The Happy Prince (B)
Richard Wright: Black Boy (B)
Karen Blixen: Out of Africa (C)
Tim Bowler: Storm Catchers (C)
Roald Dahl: Edward the Conqueror and Other Stories (C)
Charles Dickens: A Christmas Carol (C)
Sir Arthur Conan Doyle: The Hound of the Baskervilles (C)
Graham Greene: The Third Man (C)
James Heneghan: Safe House (C)
S.E. Hinton: Tex (C)
Ira Levin: Rosemary's Baby (C)
James Moloney: Gracey (C)
Celia Rees: Witch Child (C)
Mary Shelley: Frankenstein (C)
Alexander McCall Smith: Tears of the Giraffe (C)
R. L. Stevenson: Treasure Island (C)
Bram Stoker: Dracula (C)
Oscar Wilde: The Picture of Dorian Gray (C)
F. Scott Fitzgerald: The Great Gatsby (D)
Alan Sillitoe: The Loneliness of the Long Distance Runner (D)
R. L. Stevenson: Dr. Jekyll and Mr. Hyde (D)
Kurt Vonnegut: Slaughterhouse-Five (D)

ADULT:
Peter James: The Perfect Murder (B)
Stephen Speight: Doomed to Die (B)
Stephen Speight: Swindled (B)
Minette Walters: Chickenfeed (C)